Henry Houseworth

Another wonder in heaven;

As interpreted by means of gospel equivalents, according to the principles

of Scriptural algebra

Henry Houseworth

Another wonder in heaven;
As interpreted by means of gospel equivalents, according to the principles of Scriptural algebra

ISBN/EAN: 9783337713973

Printed in Europe, USA, Canada, Australia, Japan

Cover: Foto ©ninafisch / pixelio.de

More available books at **www.hansebooks.com**

Another Wonder

IN HEAVEN;

AS INTERPRETED BY MEANS OF

GOSPEL EQUIVALENTS,

ACCORDING TO THE

PRINCIPLES OF SCRIPTURAL ALGEBRA.

BY HENRY HOUSEWORTH,

AUTHOR OF THE "FEDERURBIAN SCHOOL BOOKS," AND "THE DAWN OF REVELATION UNVEILED."

CINCINNATI:
PRINTED AND BOUND FOR THE AUTHOR BY THE
ELM STREET PRINTING CO., 176 ELM ST.
1868.

Entered according to Act of Congress, in the year 1868, by
HENRY HOUSEWORTH,
In the Clerk's Office of the District Court of the United States, for the Southern District of Ohio.

CONTENTS.

CHAPTER I.
Another Wonder in Heaven.................................. Page 11

CHAPTER II.
The Two Witnesses... 24

CHAPTER III.
The Four Living Creatures..................................... 30

CHAPTER IV.
The Seven Seals.. 49

CHAPTER V.
The Last Seven Plagues... 83
Conclusion.. 109

CIRCULAR.

To all, who fear God and work righteousness, the author sendeth greeting.

DEARLY BELOVED:

I PRESENT you a treatise on "THE LAST SEVEN PLAGUES," entitled "ANOTHER WONDER IN HEAVEN." It issues from the press unattended with the banner of any religious denomination. This fact, and the subject of which it treats, make it a lone and solitary stranger. A stranger it acknowledges itself to be, but not an alien or an enemy. For it professes to belong to the fellow citizens of the saints, and of the household of God. You know your duty to strangers. "Be not forgetful to entertain strangers, for some have entertained angels unawares. And he that giveth a cup of cold water to a disciple shall not lose his reward. Prove all things, and hold fast that which is good."

This book is the result of a dream, which, about eight years ago, excited a curiosity to investigate the book of Revelation by means of gospel equivalents. The interpretation corresponds with the nature of the dream. And all parts of the dream have been fulfilled except the last, which is the reward of so protracted an effort under discouraging circumstances. The opportunity to revise and prepare the manuscript for the press was afforded during the lonely hours of night, while watching at the bedside of an afflicted child, who was returned to her paternal roof despairing of conjugal felicity and every other human joy. The profits of this book, if any, will be devoted (as long as shall be necessary) to cheer her in her earthly pilgrimage. A word to the wise is sufficient.

INTRODUCTION.

The primary object of writing this book is to verify the declaration of Scripture which saith: "The testimony of the Lord is sure, making wise the simple." To show that it is sure in its interpretation as well as in the fulfillment of prophecy. To show that the interpretation of Scripture is capable of being reduced to a mathematical certainty.

The object is also to show that all Scripture, given by inspiration of God, is profitable. That a special blessing is conferred by reading, hearing, and keeping the words recorded in the book of Revelation. And that that book is not a sealed book, but whoever discards it as useless, is calling that a mystery which God calls a revelation, and is also, by his example, disobeying the command given to John, namely: "Seal not the sayings of the prophecy of this book." And whoever puts obstructions in the way of any one who labors by his time, and means to show the utility of that book, is disobeying the command: "Bear ye one another's burdens, and thus fulfill the law of Christ."

Let us follow the example of the Bereans, who searched the Scriptures to see if these things were so. Because it is written in Dan. xii. 4: "Many shall run to and fro, and knowledge shall be increased."

Nor have we reason to suppose that that prophecy is entirely fulfilled in the increase of those natural sciences which chiefly promote bodily ease and enjoyment. For it is also written in Jeremiah xxxi. 34: "And they shall teach no more every man his neighbor, and every man his brother, saying: "Know the Lord: for they shall all know me, from the least of them unto the greatest of them, saith the Lord." All prophecies of Scripture must be fulfilled. And it is recorded in Rev. x. 7: "But in the days of the voice of the seventh angel, when he shall begin to sound, the mystery of God should be finished, as he has declared to his servants the prophets." And it is maintained that this auspicious day is now dawning upon the Christian world.

CHAPTER I.

ANOTHER WONDER IN HEAVEN.

"And I saw another sign in heaven, great and marvelous, seven angels having the seven last plagues; for in them is filled up the wrath of God."—Rev. xv. 1.

ANOTHER implies one or more previous to it. Accordingly, I find that there are other signs or wonders mentioned in Rev. xii. For the same word in the Greek is variously rendered sign or wonder. The first is the woman clothed with the sun. And the second is the great red dragon. And that we may have a better understanding of the third, which is the chief subject of this treatise, I will briefly interpret the first and second in the order in which they occur. The first mentioned is in Rev. xii. 1: "And there appeared a great wonder in heaven; a woman clothed with the sun, and the moon under her feet, and upon her head a crown of twelve stars." The solution of this figure, according to the algebraic application of gospel equivalents, makes it represent the church of Christ arrayed as the bride adorned for her husband with the Mosaic dispensation upon which to stand, and the gospel radiating its light from her person, as the sun shineth in his glory, and the teachings of the twelve apostles as bright stars to illuminate her crown of glory.

In elucidating the figure—a woman clothed with the sun, it will be necessary to ascertain what is meant by the word sun. It is recorded in Mal. iv. 2: "But unto you that fear my name shall the Sun of righteousness arise with healing in his wings." This is generally understood to refer to Christ. The phrase " of righteousness" is only explanatory, and does not alter the meaning. The comparison of Christ to the sun is also shown by his transfiguration recorded in Matt. xvii. 2: "And his face did shine as the sun, and his raiment was white as the light." And this agrees, also, with the description given of him recorded in Rev. i. 16, "and his countenance was as the sun shineth in his strength." From this scriptural testimony, I suppose it will be seen that Christ is equivalent to sun, and the words Christ and sun may be substituted for each other, whenever additional clearness of idea will result from the operation. And, therefore, to be clothed with the sun is equivalent to being clothed with the sun of righteousness, with the robe of Christ's righteousness, or with Christ himself. According as it is written: They that are baptized into Christ have put on Christ. To put on denotes the act of clothing, or being clothed. The next unknown figure to be ascertained is the word moon, which was under her feet. I have already shown that Christ was the sun or sun of righteousness. It becomes now necessary to find another gospel equivalent for sun or Christ, which will bear a superior relation to the unknown value or signification of moon. And the equivalent necessary to solve the next unknown signification will prove to be the gospel, which is shown to be equivalent to Christ. Because to preach Christ is to preach the gospel. It is recorded in John i. 17: "For the law was given by Moses, but grace and truth came by Jesus Christ." For the present I shall assume that the phrase "grace and truth" are equivalent to the word gospel. If so, the algebraic substitution of the word gospel for the phrase "grace and truth," we have a new declaration, the law was given by Moses, but the gospel came by Jesus Christ. And it is obvious that the law given by Moses was the next inferior dispensation to the gospel. It then bears the same relation to the gospel as the moon in the natural world does to the sun. The moon, then, that was under her feet was the law of Moses.

But that this substitution of equivalents shall not merely rest on the assumption that the phrase "grace and truth" is equivalent to the word gospel, I shall endeavor to prove that the phrase means exactly the gospel—nothing more and nothing less. In algebraic language grace and truth may be considered bound together by a vinculum. For the signification of the two words must be combined. And hence the declaration becomes true, that truth is all the word of God, but grace and truth is only a part of it, which may be seen thus: A noun without an article, or other restrictive word or phrase to limit it, is generally taken in its widest sense. A candid temper is proper for man, that is all mankind. A man is any man, but only one man taken without distinction from the mass. A man of learning is one man, who may be selected from all the learned class, which is more limited. A man of learning and piety must be selected from the learned and pious, which still restricts and diminishes the class. So, also, grace and truth, are so much of truth or of the word of God as is a grace or favor, and includes only the gospel. For the law given to Adam was not a favor, but the natural result of his relation to his Creator.

But the gospel was a favor purchased by the blood of Christ.

I have asserted that truth is all the word of God. For it is written in John xvii. 17: "Sanctify them through thy truth: thy word is truth. Thy word is all the word of God, a part of which is a favor, and a part not. It, therefore, becomes necessary to substract law at his mouth: "For he is the messenger of the Lord of hosts."—Mal. ii. 7. A pastor is the priest of the gospel dispensation, and a messenger is an angel. Things that are equal to the same are equal to each other. Therefore, the seven angels are the pastors of the seven churches of Asia.

"Which stood before God." The seven stars are represented to be held in Christ's right hand. He is represented as standing at the golden altar before the throne. And, moreover, Christ is represented in Rev. i. 13, as being in the midst of the seven golden candlesticks. And in verse twentieth, the seven candle sticks are declared to be the seven churches. A pastor's business and duties are with his flock or church. And if Christ was in the midst of the golden candlesticks, and his place was at the golden altar before the throne, and the seven stars were in his right hand, they, also, must be situated before the throne of God.

"And to them were given seven trumpets." The trumpet is an instrument of publication or proclamation; as is also a book. They are, therefore, equivalents. The seven trumpets are the seven copies of the book of Revelation, which John was commanded to write and send to the churches of Asia. According as it is written, "What thou seest, write in a book and send it unto the seven churches which are in Asia."—Rev. i. 11. They were to declare the contents of the book, like as if they proclaimed them with a trumpet. According as it is written in Isa. lviii. 1: "Cry aloud, spare not, lift up thy voice as a trumpet, and show my people their transgression, and the house of Jacob their sins."

Rev. viii. 3: "And another angel came and stood at the altar, having a golden censer; and there was given unto him much incense, that he should offer it with the prayers of all saints upon the golden altar which was before the throne." The golden censer, golden altar, and the incense with the prayers of all saints are the names of things and persons in both the Old and New Testaments. They, therefore, need not be solved by gospel equivalents, or take from the whole word of God so much as is not a favor or grace, in order to make the remainder a favor or grace. But if a part were taken away, what remains must be less than the whole before any was taken therefrom. Therefore, grace and truth combined must be less than truth alone. And this combination is nothing else than the gospel. For the gospel is a favor, and the chief part of the truth or word of God. Because all other parts were written to substantiate and enforce its principles and duties.

Now the gospel is compared with law given by Moses. But I have shown that Christ is the sun of righteousness, and to preach Christ is to preach the gospel. Therefore, the sun of righteousness or the gospel is compared to the law of Moses, and is greater than it. Now, the next inferior light to the sun in the natural world is the moon, which, therefore, represents the law of Moses. And if Christ or the gospel is the sun, and the law of Moses is the moon, the teachings of the twelve apostles are the stars which adorn the head of the woman clothed with the sun. She is the Lamb's wife, the Christian Church, prepared as a bride adorned for her husband. Her husband is king of kings, and lord of lords. She must, therefore, wear a crown. But of what is her crown composed. The moon or the Mosaic dispensation is the foundation upon which she stands. For the church is built upon the foundation of the apostles and prophets—Jesus Christ, himself, being the chief corner-stone. The prophets are included in the Mosaic dispensation, which is a foundation beneath her feet. The sun, which is the bright apparel of this bride, is the gospel as taught by the four evangelists, which is proved to be true by the prophecies concerning Christ, recorded in the Old Testament. And the teachings and recorded practice of the twelve apostles are necessary to crown the whole, to make the church a queen worthy of her husband and lord.

As the moon in the natural world receives its light from the sun, so, also, the Mosaic dispensation shines with light reflected from the gospel. Moses and Christ were both lawgivers, and, as such, were superior to the apostles, who were not endowed with that dignity. Yet their teachings were bright lights to enlighten what would otherwise be comparatively dark and obscure in the moral and religious world.

But it may be asked how can the church, which is organized on earth, be called a wonder in heaven? To this it is replied that the church of Christ is a wonder to the angels of heaven and to the inhabitants of earth. For it is written, the angels desire to look into it. They desire to contemplate the plan of salvation, and rejoice over one sinner that repenteth. It is also a wonder to the redeemed who constitute the kingdom of heaven on earth. In other words, it is a wonder in the kingdom of heaven or gospel dispensation. According as it is written, the kingdom of heaven is at hand, meaning the gospel dispensation. For it commences on earth, and ends in the glorified state of the redeemed in heaven. And as the gospel dispensation, the heaven spoken of in the text, has its primary organization on earth, so, also, it is a wonder to the wicked, both angels and men. According as it is written, the devils believe and tremble, which is doing more than is done by wicked men. For it is written in Acts xiii. 41: "For I work a work in your days, a work which ye shall in nowise believe, though a man declare it unto you." And the Jews are a standing monument of unbelief. The organization of the Christian Church and the fulfillment of the prophecies concerning it were too wonderful for their acceptance and belief.

THE SECOND WONDER IN HEAVEN.

It is recorded in Rev. xii. 3: "And there appeared another wonder in heaven; and behold a great red dragon, having seven heads and ten horns, and seven crowns upon his heads."

This wonder is two-fold, namely: spiritual and temporal. The spirit or soul of this great red dragon is Satan himself breathing into, and giving life and vigor to a political organization among men, which for ages has worked out his diabolical purposes. It is wonderful why Satan, possessing angelic powers, and seeing the unveiled glory of the Almighty should so far forget his duty and interest as to rebel against his righteous government. And it is also wonderful that in after ages the spirit of evil should employ agents, and centralize his power to seek conquests from the followers of the Lamb. And it is equally due to his malignity and perseverance that he should establish his sway to so great an extent as to obtain prominent places in the earth as the seat of his dominion. The Roman empire, the body wherein dwelt the spirit of evil, seated upon the seven-hilled city, persecuting the church of the Most High was a wonder in many respects. It was terrible to its enemies in the day of battle, and in its infancy magnanimous to its captured enemies, but unrelenting in its persecutions of

Christianity. The second wonder exhibits the malignity of Paganism and irreligion as opposed to Christianity. It is the wrath of man. But the third wonder is greater as it compriseth the wrath of God.

ANOTHER WONDER IN HEAVEN.

It is recorded in Rev. xv. 1: "And I saw another sign in heaven, great and marvelous, seven angels having the seven last plagues; for in them is filled up the wrath of God." The third wonder in heaven, or in the gospel dispensation exhibits God's special protection of his church, and his providential care in overruling the evil passions of men to build up his church on earth. It is wonderful that men possessing the will and, apparently, the ability to defeat some prophecies should be deterred from so doing without any apparent constraint. And this only exhibits the great power and glory of God, in concealing from men so much of his purposes as they would be disposed to defeat, if they knew them. And, again, it is wonderful that he should dictate a book which should be the conclusion of all prophecies, and yet only so much of it be understood in different ages of the world as would be conducive to his glory and accomplish his designs.

The last seven plagues is a wonder on many accounts. It is a wonder that the book of Revelation, which contains an account of them, should not be thoroughly understood until they are completed. This fact is in accordance with the prophecy concerning them. The book which contains an account of them is properly called a Revelation, and John was commanded not to seal the sayings of the prophecy of this book. And this book I understand to be that little open book which John was told to eat. It was, in his mouth, sweet as honey, but after it was eaten it was bitter. So men have thought this book to be a glowing picture of heavenly bliss, but, when fully understood, I think it proves to be a lesson of earthly duty, and a prophecy of calamity to the human race. Like as the temple of the tabernacle of the testimony in heaven was opened, and no man was able to enter into the temple till the seven plagues of the seven angels were fulfilled. So, also, with the prophecy of the last seven plagues fully declared to men; and all the principles of interpretation fully understood; no man has heretofore so combined those principles as to make them available to interpret that book. And if this interpretation is correct, what has baffled the mightiest intellects possessing ponderous volumes of theological lore and lives of leisure to read them, if the providence of God is introduced in a manner that appears accidental by wayfaring men, destitute of profound biblical attainments? Well may the inspired penman designate the last seven plagues as another sign or wonder in heaven, or the gospel dispensation, great and marvelous. For in them is filled up the wrath of God. For the complete outpouring of the last seven plagues constitutes a prophetic epoch in the history of the world, because it closes up an administration of displeasure and wrath, and introduces one of mercy and benignity.

CHAPTER II.

THE TWO WITNESSES.

The knowledge which mankind have of the last seven plagues is primarily and chiefly derived from the word of God, contained in the book of Revelation. For, although it might be possible for man, after the accomplishment of those plagues upon the inhabitants of the earth, to see and acknowledge the dispensation of God in those judgments, yet it is highly probable they would not have classified them into seven divisions, nor have had very clear ideas of their design and results. In illustrating the subject, therefore, the introductory evidence must be chiefly derived from the word of God. But the final development of the subject, or the identification of the last seven plagues, severally, admits of collateral evidence taken from authentic history, whether human or divine. There are, therefore, two witnesses graciously afforded us, so that, by their united testimony, every word shall be established. These are the two witnesses mentioned in Rev. xi. 3, who should prophecy twelve hundred and sixty days, clothed in sackcloth. For these witnesses are not the Old and New Testaments, as some suppose. The union of the latter constitute the testimony of one witness, which is the written word of God. For, as in the natural world, day and night constitute one legal day, or, as the Scriptures declare, the evening and the morning were the first day. So, also, the evidence of the brighter light of the gospel, and the inferior light of the Mosaic dispensation constitute the written testimony of one witness. And as the laws of men are divided into two kinds, the written and the unwritten law, so, also, God's will or law to man is made known by his written law, or the Bible, and by his unwritten law, which is contained in his works of creation and providence. "For the invisible things of him from the creation of the world are clearly seen, being understood by the things that are made, even his eternal power and Godhead, so that they are without excuse."—Rom. i. 20. Our knowledge of God's will is derived from the book of Inspiration and the book of Providence. The book of Inspiration usually affords us the general proposition or truth, which we have to carry out in detail. And our minds are assisted in this effort by the book of Providence, which affords us the details, which have to be generalized. The agreement of these two sources of information is the highest evidence attainable by man. For one is the infallible teachings of God's word, and the other is the undeniable history of the past.

In referring you to the scriptural authority for the use of two witnesses, I will mention, first, the one who is spoken of in Rev. i. 5: "And from Jesus Christ, who is the faithful witness and the first begotten of the dead." To his testimony you will make no objection. He is the author and finisher of our faith. And as our system of faith is taught in the

Scriptures you will receive them as the testimony of Jesus Christ. Moreover, Christ is declared to be the Word of God, as we also acknowledge the Scriptures to be. Therefore, the Bible is one of the witnesses, which I suppose will be received as such accordingly. For you may notice that the Scriptures and the word of God are equivalent, meaning the same book. And as Christ is declared to be the word of God, therefore, if Christ is the faithful witness, the Scriptures are also; especially as they are his written testimony. And as human laws admit oral or spoken testimony, so, also, the depositions or written testimony of witnesses that are absent.

The other witness, by whose testimony I undertake to prove the identity of the last seven plagues, is the book of Providence, containing the designs and will of God, as revealed in history. It is recorded in Rom. i. 20: "For the invisible things of him from the creation of the world are clearly seen, being understood by the things that are made, even his eternal power and Godhead." It is also declared in

Scripture, by their fruits ye shall know them. So, also, the reason of human law supposes that every intelligent being designs the inevitable consequences of his acts. For if a rational man should present a pistol to your breast, and demand your money or your life, and, if in failing to receive the former, he takes the latter, the laws of men presume that he intended murder. But this rule of interpreting design or intention is not confined to man alone, but is true in regard to all intelligences, whether man, the angelic hosts of light or darkness, and, also, in regard to the great Supreme Ruler of all intelligences. For it is written, he doeth his will among the armies of heaven, and among the inhabitants of earth. Now, if we can ascertain by any means what God doeth, we can also ascertain his will. For he doeth his will. It would not, of course, be proper to attribute anything to the Supreme Being as his work, unless it corresponds with his attributes of wisdom, justice and benevolence.

But results corresponding to these attributes have been known to proceed from the defeated projects of wicked and malicious men. The religious world have not feared to attribute such results to God's special Providence. These in detail, one after another, have been attributed to our benevolent Creator. But none, to my knowledge, have seen fit to generalize these detached works attributed to God as his work, and from them show his design or will. Yet such repeated results give as unmistakable evidence of design in the moral world, as does the uniformity of the laws of nature show God's design in them. I presume what is acknowledged to be true in detail, will not be denied when combined in a general form. So, I conclude, that the works of Providence will be allowed as a competent witness, and will constitute the second witness by which the propositions of this book will be proved.

CHAPTER III.

THE FOUR LIVING CREATURES.

It is recorded in Rev. xv. 7, 8: "And one of the four beasts gave unto the seven angels seven golden vials full of the wrath of God, who liveth forever and ever. And the temple was filled with smoke from the glory of God, and from his power; and no man was able to enter into the temple, till the seven plagues of the seven angels were fulfilled."

The correct identification of the four living creatures, as the phrase "the four beasts" might more properly be translated, gives the proper clew, as I believe, to the unfolding of all the mysteries of the book of Revelation. For, although it might be possible to have a proper understanding of those personages, and yet be able to solve but few of the mysteries of that book. Yet, if they are not correctly ascertained, it is, as I suppose, impossible to have correct views of the figurative expressions contained in that book. They hold conspicuous stations in the kingdom of heaven or gospel dispensation; and may, therefore, be supposed to be holy men or holy angels. But if it can be proved that they belong to the human family, we may reasonably look for them in familiar personages, described in inspired or human history.

' These four living creatures appear to be leaders of, and superior in station to, the four and twenty elders. For the latter seem to obey their direction. For it is written in Rev. iv. 9: "And when those beasts give glory and honor and thanks to him that sat on the throne, who liveth forever and ever, the four and twenty elders fall down before him that sat on the throne, and worship him that liveth forever and ever." Their number being four, does not allow us to identify them with Peter and Paul, individually or collectively, as holding chief supremacy in the church, the kingdom of heaven, or the gospel dispensation. Nor do we appear authorized to look to the Old Testament dispensation for the identification of these personages called the four beasts or living creatures. For it is written in Matt. xi. 9, 11: "What went ye out for to see? A prophet? yea, I say unto you, and more than a prophet. Verily I say unto you, among them that are born of women there hath not risen a greater than John the Baptist: notwithstanding, he that is least in the kingdom of heaven is greater than he." If the four and twenty elders are apostles and prophets, because the church is built on the testimony of the apostles and prophets, there would seem to be no other distinguished personages left who could occupy so conspicuous a station, unless they were the four evangelists. These correspond in their number, in the equality of their office, and in the superiority of the station they occupy. And the figurative description of them, unitedly and severally, seems to show the duties and importance of their social position.

If the four beasts or living creatures are the

four evangelists, the one that gave to the seven angels the seven golden vials full of the wrath of God, was John the Revelator, who was also one of the evangelists. The book of Revelation asserts that John the Revelator wrote this book unto the seven churches of Asia. The word angel means messenger. And it is recorded in Mal. ii. 7: "For the priest's lips should keep knowledge. For he is the messenger of the Lord of hosts." The gospel equivalent for gold is wisdom, and for golden is wise, which may be seen in the following manner: Wisdom is more precious than rubies, and the gold of Ophir can not be compared unto it. Although it is said that the gold of Ophir can not be compared unto it, nevertheless, by comparison, gold is declared to be inferior to it, but is the most valuable substance in the material world, as wisdom is the most precious in the moral and intellectual world. It is, therefore, the only equivalent that can be found for wisdom, and is used in all the passages of Revelation as its equivalent. We must, therefore, conclude that the golden vials which contained the seven last plagues were the seven copies of the book of Revelation, dictated by divine wisdom, and sent to the seven churches of Asia. This book contained the prophecy of these plagues, which was sufficient guarantee of their fulfillment. The seven pastors of the seven churches of Asia may, therefore, be said to have received the container of those plagues which the vials are, when they received the book which contained the prophecy of those plagues. For God's word shall not return unto him void, but shall accomplish that whereunto it was sent.

But as I have, for the sake of convenience, only supposed that the four beasts or living creatures were the four evangelists, it becomes necessary to produce further evidence in support of that opinion. So, then, I undertake, first, to prove by the Scriptures that they belong to the human family. And, secondly, I shall produce the gospel equivalents to exhibit their individual characteristics, by which they are designated in the Scriptures; as Matthew, the publican or tax-gatherer; Mark, the brief writer; Luke, the accomplished scholar; and John, the bosom companion of our Lord, descending to the grave in peace. These are more sure and certain representations than if designated by their names or bodily features.

That these four beasts or living creatures belong to the human family, is evident from Rev. v. 8, 9: "And when he had taken the book, the four beasts and four and twenty elders fell down before the Lamb, having every one of them harps, and golden vials full of odors, which are the prayers of saints. And they sung a new song, saying, Thou art worthy to take the book, and to open the seal thereof: for thou wast slain, and hast redeemed us to God by thy blood out of every kindred, and tongue, and people, and nation." Christ was made under the law, to redeem those who were under the law. And we have no account of any, but the human race, that have been redeemed. And this is also supported by the testimony of Rev. xiv. 3: " And they sung as it were a new song before the throne, and before the four beasts, and the elders; and no man could learn that song but the hundred and forty and four thousand, which were redeemed from the earth." From the last testimony it is evident that none but the redeemed could learn that song; and from the first testimony, that the four beasts or living creatures, and the four and twenty elders actually joined in that song. The song, in both instances, is called a new song, and is, therefore, presumed to be the same. It was the song of the redeemed—of the four and twenty elders, and of the one hundred and forty and four thousand, which were sealed of all the tribes of the children of Israel, and of a great multitude, which no man could number of all nations, and kindreds, and people, and tongues, who had come out of great tribulation, and had washed their robes, and made them white in the blood of the Lamb. This new song was, doubtless, joined in conjointly by them all, although the four living creatures, and the four and twenty elders, taken separately from the rest, may not have been of every kindred, and tongue, and people, and nation. The four beasts, and the four and twenty elders consequently belonged to the human family. Angels could not learn that song, for they could not, with propriety, say what was not true. For angels were never redeemed. Wicked angels never received, and holy angels never needed, redemption. We can not, therefore, look for the four beasts or living creatures among the angels of light. And the angels of darkness have no desire to be placed so near the throne of God and the Lamb. Now, these four living creatures hold a conspicuous part in the kingdom, which is represented by the throne and the seats of the elders. And, as they belong to the human family, we must, consequently, look for them among some who have held important offices in the kingdom of grace. And, accordingly, the four evangelists occupy that position in regard to other men. And although I can not produce direct Scripture testimony calling these four living creatures the four evangelists, yet I expect to prove by the established characteristics of animated nature, by which they are represented, and the scriptural usage of the same, that they identically represent the biographical characteristics of these four evangelists, found recorded in the sacred Scriptures. And especially do I expect it to be fully apparent, after quoting numerous passages from the writings of these evangelists, which will prove what is set forth on the opening of the four seals, when the four beasts or living creatures are represented to say, "come and see." For it is a remarkable coincidence, that numerous passages introduced in their connection with the words "come and see" should precisely disclose the picture or representation exhibited by the opening of the seals, recorded in the sixth chapter. This coincidence is very apparent—is at least beautiful—and to my mind affords evidence of inspired design. Nor have I, among the numerous individuals to whom I have exhibited this coincidence, met a person, learned or unlearned, who denied its efficacy or beauty.

The four beasts agree in this particular, namely, in having eyes before and behind. Eyes denote wisdom; and before and behind denote the future and the past. The four evangelists agree in the possession and distribution of knowledge of future and past transactions. History and prophecy are some of the means used by the sacred penmen to diffuse divine wisdom. And these are conspicuous in the four evangelists. Although all the holy men of God, in inditing the sacred Scriptures, spake as they were moved by the Holy Ghost; yet, in so doing, they did not lose their identity, or distinguishable traits of character. The disciples of Christ were called from various pursuits of life, and under various circumstances. And in their intercourse with other men, whether in speaking or writing, they still retained their peculiarities of style or manner. As it is recorded, that John came neither eating nor drinking, and the Son of man came eating and drinking, yet wisdom is justified of her children. So, also, the peculiarities of the four evangelists are represented to us under four distinct and easy distinguishable traits, namely, by imagery taken from the savage and domestic state—from the celestial and terrestrial spheres.

"And the first beast was like a lion, and the second beast like a calf, and the third beast had a face as a man, and the fourth beast was like a flying eagle."—Rev. iv. 7. The first beast or living creature, therefore, will be Matthew, who, when he was called to be a disciple, was found sitting at the receipt of custom. This was the tax-gatherer's or treasurer's office. For custom is tax; as we say the custom-house at which duties on foreign goods are collected. Matthew is repeatedly denominated in the Scriptures the publican. He is, therefore, distinguished as the servant of the Roman empire in the collection of taxes. And as the lion was the king of beasts, so, also, the Roman empire was king of nations, demanding its tribute, if necessary, by force. And as it is said, ye take my life when ye take the means by which I live. And the humblest tax-gatherer, in the legal discharge of his duty, was virtually supported by the entire power of the Roman empire. For if resistance should be made, sufficient force would be called out to overcome it. And no other officer of the Roman empire could bear so great a resemblance to the lion, which is king of beasts, as would the more humble tax-gatherer or publican.

The second beast or living creature, namely, Mark, is represented to us under the figure of a calf. It is apparent that brevity and omission are distinguishable traits of Mark's style of writing, which all good judges would be ready to admit. But some might not be willing to admit a similar trait in the natural characteristic of the calf. Admitting that other animals in the natural world skip as well as the calf, yet, perhaps, none do so in a more remarkable degree; or are as directly so described by the pen of inspiration. Be that as it may, it is sufficient for me to know that that characteristic is applied to the calf either by the acknowledged opinion of men, or by the positive declaration of Scripture. The substitution of the natural equivalent of skipping as a prominent characteristic of the calf, for the hasty glancing style of Mark's composition, is not the only evidence of his being the second beast or living creature. For it is supported by the collateral evidence derived from the use of the words "come and see" as an index to a subject before hidden, but then made known, as will be further seen on the opening of the second seal.

The natural idea attached to a calf may be in the opinion of some contemptible. Yet this is not necessarily the true scriptural idea. For we are assisted in our definition of a calf by divine inspiration. As it is recorded in Psalms xxix. 5, 6: "The voice of the Lord breaketh the cedars of Lebanon; he maketh them also to skip like a calf." So we see that the idea attached to the calf is that of skipping. And we have often admired the skipping of the calf, which shows its agility and strength. And as the calf in its vigor skips over the ground, so, also, the second evangelist, in his haste to introduce us without delay to the important design and teachings of Christ, skips over the record of his birth and parentage. This omission was not essential, as the other evangelists amply illustrated that subject. And this may have been done for another reason, namely, to teach us an important lesson in interpreting the Scriptures, which is, that many other things were said and done by Christ and his disciples, which were not written. So in the interpretation of the Scriptures by the method herein developed, this rule continually presents itself for our consideration.

The third beast or living creature, which we assert to be Luke, is said to have " a face as a man." The phrase, " a face as a man," is peculiarly adapted to express his exalted condition. That the natural position of the face of man denotes his elevated character, is evident from the humility and dejection which is expressed by its prostration. As may be seen by its use in the Sacred Scriptures; for we find that others, and Christ himself, in times of deepest humility and distress, prostrated their faces to the ground. To have a face as a man appears to us in a two-fold light: First, as superior to other living creatures, inasmuch as man is superior to all animate creation. Secondly, having "a face as a man" as a personal trait does not make him distinguishable from other men. Such apparently opposite personal characteristics can not be reconciled in any other evangelist than Luke. For he was superior to the other evangelists in the extent of his acquired abilities. He is styled the beloved physician, and was, doubtless, versed in medical science. And we need no further proof of his literary attainments than the original copy of the book of Luke. It is known to all Greek scholars that the writer of the book of Luke is the only evangelist who does not exhibit multiplied proofs of their Hebrew origin, as plainly as common people of foreign birth exhibit their various nationalities; as a Scotch, German, or Irishman may be known by their respective peculiarities of words, phrases, or pronunciation. So, also, Luke, in being a better Greek scholar than the other evangelists, excelled them even as "a face as a man" is superior to the rest of animated nature. And, at the same time, his nationality, or the era of his writings, is not discernible by his style, national words, or phrases. The other evangelists, in writing the words of inspiration, were not overruled in expressing those ideas in their own Hebrew dialect of the Greek language. And these circumstances afford incontestable proof to Greek scholars of all ages and countries, that Matthew, Mark and John were Hebrews, writing near the time of Augustus Cæsar in the Greek language. This, at least, establishes their identity and nationality, and gives mankind a better opportunity to judge of their truthfulness or veracity. And Luke's differing from the other evangelists is rather corroborative of their testimony than otherwise, as it forms a contrast which can only be accounted for from the fact that he was a Gentile, and one of the early fruits of the promulgation of the gospel to the Gentile world. So, in elucidating the glowing figures presented by the Revelator, we are obliged to present to our minds and the minds of others, who hear or read our elucidation, some of the most important evidences of the genuineness of the gospels, and with them of the writings of both the Old and New Testaments; for they are all connected, and if the gospels are true or false, the other writings of the Scriptures stand or fall with them. This, alone, is sufficient vindication of the wisdom and design of such a figurative representation. Truly, it is said, Christ is the power of God and the wisdom of God. For such figures are like the finger of God, pointing out to us the most incontestible evidence of the truthfulness of the gospels, and of the whole divine record.

"And the fourth beast was like a flying eagle." It should be noticed that the eagle is not here represented to us in its capacity of a bird of prey. Therefore, it would be improper to identify it with Matthew the publican, or any other servant of the Roman empire, whether civil, political, or military, but as the king of birds, flying loftily in the sky, and apparently approaching nearer the sun, the ruler of day, than any other of the feathered tribe, it may well represent the evangelist John. For who, during the ministry of our Savior approached nearer his person than the beloved disciple, who, according to the ancient mode of taking their meals, almost reclined upon his bosom. And the resemblance between the natural sun and the sun of righteousness will not, I suppose, be disputed. For Christ is called the true light which lighteth every man that cometh into the world. Moreover, the idea attached in the Scriptures to the flying of an eagle is its ability to escape danger. As may be seen by consulting its use in Rev. xii. 14: "And to the woman were given two wings of a great eagle, that she might fly into the wilderness," which was to her a place of safety. And this ability to escape danger was granted to the evangelist John, which is not recorded of any other. For it is recorded in John xxi. 23: "Yet Jesus said not unto him, he shall not die; but, if I will that he tarry till I come, what is that to thee?" Which is generally understood to signify that he should escape the power of all persecutions, and die a natural death.

It is, therefore, maintained that these four beasts or living creatures, who hold so conspicuous a station around the throne of the kingdom of heaven or gospel dispensation, in their primary interpretation, denote the four evangelists personally, and in their secondary, their writings or the gospels of our Savior Jesus Christ. They are understood to be the same as the four angels standing on the four corners of the earth, mentioned in Rev. vii. But the explanation of that scriptural passage comes not within the scope of this presnt treatise. They are also understood to be the same as the four angels bound in the great river Euphrates mentioned in Rev. ix. 14. The elucidation of which is connected with the outpouring of the sixth vial, in the consideration of which some remarks may be made thereon.

CHAPTER IV.

THE SEVEN SEALS.

It is recorded in Rev. v. i: "And I saw in the right hand of him that sat on the throne a book, written within and on the back side, sealed with seven seals."

There is a peculiarity attending the interpretation of the prophecy in the book of Revelation that should be noticed, which is, that the representation is such as an intelligent human being might arrive at on contemplating the subject retrospectively without the aid of divine inspiration. This may be termed the human aspect of affairs described, or judging from appearances. Other parts of Scripture more frequently present to us the divine aspect of the subject expressed, or the real state of the case as viewed by angels or the divine intelligence by the light of eternity. This difference does not arise from the different methods used in the interpretation of the Scriptures, but from the different manners in which they were written. Both aspects or views of inspiration are useful in their different places. And one reason that the divine aspect of affairs is more frequently given in other parts of the Scriptures may be that the human aspect is more easily supplied from human sources of knowledge, and is not so important in retrospective history. For men can easily write the history of the past as they understand it. So, also, in prophesying of the future, it seems more necessary to describe affairs according to appearances, so that when the fulfillment takes place, men may the more easily discern it.

The better to illustrate the subject, I will briefly announce what book it was that was sealed with seven seals, and show the result of the seven seals opened, together with the manner of their opening. The fifth chapter of the book of this prophecy represents that the Old

THE SEVEN SEALS. 53

Testament, at least in seven particulars, would be a perfect failure without the aid of the New. That neither men nor angels could fully comprehend its design or utility without the additional light, either by direct or reflected illumination of the New Testament dispensation. But with that additional source of comprehension, it was an object of rejoicing to all wise and good intelligences. Six seals are opened in the sixth chapter of the book of this prophecy, as follows: The first is, that Christ, under the most trying and critical circumstances, should give indubitable evidence of the purity of his character, and his resistance of all unholy passions, and should manifest even while here in the flesh his infinite wisdom and power, and finally overcome death and the grave. The second seal opened, discloses that the Jewish temple should be destroyed, and its institutions abolished. The third seal opened, made it manifest that the Roman army was commissioned by the court of heaven to destroy the city of Jerusalem, under very extraordinary circumstances of war and famine; but were withheld by the some divine power from exercising that same cruelty upon the early Christians, who were forwarned of that calamity, and directed how to escape its evils. The fourth seal opened, disclosed the exciting cause of the persecution of the Christian martyrs, which is briefly summed up in their confession that Christ was the Son of God. For which confession, also, Christ himself, under oath before the Jewish high priest, was condemned to the death of the cross. The opening of the fifth seal disclosed the fact that the martyrs, although so brutally treated by men in authority, were held in high favor by the God of heaven, who only delayed to execute summary vengeance on their murderers, that the remnant of his people might be gathered into his kingdom. The opening of the sixth seal, made it manifest that a warlike power was raised, which threatened the mighty ones of earth with temporal devastation, desolation, and the overthrow of civil authority; but which was not permitted to carry into execution its plotted evils, until the servants of God had given incontestable proof of the purity and inoffensiveness of the Christian religion. The opening of the seventh seal discloses the threatening, and the manner of executing seven dire calamities upon the human race. It embraces the seven trumpets and the last seven plagues, and the destructive and beneficial results thereof, namely, the downfall of Babylon or the apostate church, and the renewal of the New Jerusalem, or the Church of Christ in its pristine purity and holiness.

But the way in which our attention is drawn to those declarations of the New Testament, which furnish us with those conclusions of the results of the opening of the first four seals, is seen in the following manner: It is supposed to be proved that the four beasts mentioned in chapters fourth, fifth, and sixth of this prophecy are the same as the four angels mentioned in the sixth trumpet and vial. And I shall endeavor to show, by quotations from those authors, that they exhibit the representations manifested when those living creatures say, "come and see;" or, in other words, that the passages in connection with the words "come and see," found in the four evangelists, and what John, in the Revelation said he saw, is the sum and substance of those passages found in the evangelists in connection with the words "come and see." This is a remarkable fact, whether designed by inspiration, as is here alleged, or accidental, as those who will finally discredit this theory will suppose. And this is the more remarkable as the testimony is sometimes two-fold, inasmuch as the same representation can be proved by taking the testimony from different evangelists. For it is not contradictory to the assertion that one of the four beasts said, " come and see," if another also should, under similar circumstances, give the same invitation.

It is recorded in Rev. vi. 1, 2: "And I saw when the Lamb opened one of the seals, and I heard, as it were the noise of thunder, one of the four beasts, saying, "come and see." And I saw, and behold a white horse: and he that sat on him had a bow; and a crown was given unto him: and he went forth conquering, and to conquer." It should be noticed that it is not said the first beast, but that one of the beasts said, "come and see." So you are at liberty to take the testimony from Matthew or John, as these are the only two evangelists which have the passages in connection with the words "come and see," which will fill the representation recorded in the second verse of the same chapter. "And I saw and behold a white horse: and he that sat on him had a bow; and a crown was given unto him, and he went forth conquering, and to conquer." It can be seen that the passages, whether taken from Matthew or John, refer to Christ, and delineate his earthly difficulties, and his complete success in overcoming them. The testimony from Matthew is not so copious as that from John; but I will give that testimony first. It is recorded in Matt. ii. 9: "Lo, the star, which they saw in the east went before them till it came and stood over where the young child was." The star in silent language seemed to say, "come and see," and they obeyed. "And when they were come into the house, they saw the young child with Mary his mother, and fell down, and worshiped him." Here was the great victory, the babe born in a manger receiving the adoration and princely gifts of the wise men of the east, guided by the miraculous direction of the star of Bethlehem. And the only testimony besides this just presented, which I have found in the book of Matthew, is recorded in Matt. xxviii. 6: "Come see the place where the Lord lay." When you take into consideration the circumstances of the life and death of Jesus of Nazareth, how he was crucified with malefactors, and obtained a burial in a rich man's tomb, and that even the tomb was not able to contain his body, but it broke forth from the slumbers of the grave, as the Lord of death and the grave, the victory seems complete—from the cradle to the grave he was victorious, going forth conquering, and to conquer.

But as this testimony is not very ample, and many may be disposed to doubt the coincidence between the passages in connection with the words "come and see," because, in the first instance, it was not audible words to that effect, but only the silent guidance of the star, although came and saw are only the past tense of come and see, I will, therefore, adduce more ample testimony from the book of John. According to the scriptural declaration, the last shall be first and the first last. And accordingly the first " come and see," to which I shall call your attention, is recorded in John i. 46: "And Nathaniel said unto him, can there any good thing come out of Nazareth? Philip saith unto him, come and see." Take under consideration that Jesus Christ entered his ministry under unfavorable circumstances, being considered a Nazarene, which was allied in their minds with whatever was mean and contemptible. To conquer implies difficulties to be overcome. And here was a great prejudice of the Jews to overcome, on account of the place of his residence and supposed nativity. The first " come and see" shows a difficulty to be overcome, and a partial conquest of that difficulty. The second " come and see" shows a more complete victory, as can be seen by the second quotation from the same book, which is found recorded in John iv. 29: "Come, see a man, which told me all things that ever I did: is not this the Christ?" Here is a confession of a woman who had not been a disciple of Christ, and on that account could not be suspected of deceit, acknowledging the great wisdom of Jesus of Nazareth. In this he surely conquered, proving by a disinterested witness that he possessed ample knowledge to fill that sphere which he occupied. The next "come and see" affords no evidence of his superior wisdom, but, on the contrary, would seem to imply frailty in knowledge as he acted by the direction of others, and seemed so overcome as to sympathize and weep with his afflicted friends. Yet the sequel showed his great power, when, at his bidding, he who had been dead burst forth from the fetters of the grave. This testimony is found recorded in John xi. 34: "And said, where have ye laid him? They said unto him, Lord, come and see." We have in this passage connected with the words "come and see," a history of the resurrection of

Lazarus. Christ raising him from the dead shows forth his power, and thus proves his qualifications for the ministry which he entered into under such unfavorable circumstances, as is manifested by the exclamation, "can any good come out of Nazareth?"

But if in this life he had conquered all his other difficulties, and had suffered death by the hands of his enemies, like many others had done, he might be considered a martyr to truth or righteousness, but not a conquerer. And exultation of his enemies might have appeared true, he saved others, but himself he could not save. If he had died a natural death he might have conquered all his personal enemies. If he had not died at all he might have conquered all his enemies but the grave. For to conquer implies a contest, and if he had had no contest with the grave, he could not have conquered it. And the final testimony of this his last conquest is found recorded in John xx. 27, 29. To this we are also directed by the words "come and see," or their equivalents: "Reach hither thy finger, and behold my hands; and reach hither thy hand, and thrust it into my side; and be not faithless, but believing. And Thomas answered and said unto him, my Lord and my God. Jesus saith unto him, Thomas, because thou hast seen me, thou hast believed." Our Savior calls the acts seeing, and it was, doubtless, the strongest evidence given to any of the disciples of the resurrection of Christ from the grave.

There are other "come and sees" found in the book of John, which all show forth a conquest of difficulty. They are sometimes taken singly, and sometimes by pairs. Sometimes the see is only used, but the come is implied. But it may not be necessary to multiply evidence so much as to say all that might be said on the subject. Suffice it to say that all this testimony connected with the different "come and sees," recorded in the book of John, constitutes that portion of the history of our Savior, which was a mystery to the Jews of the Old Testament dispensation. And our Savior, who was the Lamb of God, broke this seal or revealed this mystery when he performed the acts described, and caused their record to be made for succeeding generations. By the white horse we are to understand the purity of character which Christ possessed. His having a bow denotes that he has power to execute vengeance on his enemies. And his going forth conquering and to conquer denotes that he was placed under exceedingly great difficulties, all of which we have seen he overcame.

But does any one suppose that all this resemblance is accidental, and that the person on the white horse does not necessarily represent Christ? If so, it would be well to consult the testimony of inspiration. It is recorded in Rev. xix. 11, 13: "And I saw heaven opened, and behold a white horse; and he that sat upon him was called faithful and true, and in righteousness he doth judge and make war. And he was clothed with a vesture dipped in blood: and his name is called the word of God." According as it is written in John i. 14: "And the Word was made flesh, and dwelt among us, and we beheld his glory, the glory as of the only begotten of the Father, full of grace and truth." The conclusion seems to be irresistible, and it is generally admitted to be Jesus Christ. It may be acknowledged that the person on the white horse is Christ, but, at the same time, supposed that the victory mentioned is confined to the success of his cause from the foundation of Christianity to the close of time. This supposition lessens the greatness of the conquest. For when the Lord has risen, is seated on his throne of glory, and is invested with all power in heaven and on earth, the equality of the contest is greatly diminished, as is illustrated by worldly history, when it is said Cæsar conquered Pompey. The victory is greater than if he had fought with a less distinguished general and a feebler foe. And besides the latter conquest is the personal affair of the followers of Christ while upon earth, who are seated on white horses, and follow their leader, who has gone before them in his earthly career.

"And when he had opened the second seal, I heard the second beast say, 'come and see.'

And there went out another horse that was red; and power was given to him that sat thereon to take peace from the earth, and that they should kill one another: and there was given unto him a great sword."—Rev. vi. 3, 4. It is recorded in Matt. xxiv. 2: " And Jesus said unto them, See ye not all these things? verily I say unto you, There shall not be left here one stone upon another, that shall not be thrown down." This prediction of our Savior refers to the destruction of the temple at Jerusalem, which was announced to the disciples while present in the temple. It was accompanied by the invitation, "See ye not all these things." Although they were all present in the temple, yet their minds were especially directed by the interrogation to see or contemplate the buildings of the temple, and is, therefore, equivalent to the expression, " come and see." For if their minds were directed to some other object or subject, they might not notice the greatness or beauty of the buildings. All the other evangelists, who record this prediction of our Savior, introduce it in some manner by the exhortation to see or behold these things.

That the Jewish temple and its institutions should be superseded by the Christian dispensation was a mystery to the Jews; and was only disclosed by Christ to his disciples, who were enabled to comprehend its necessity and predetermined design. And this was accomplished by war, as is denoted by the red horse which John said he saw. As the taking away peace from the earth, and having a great sword, also plainly apply.

"And when he opened the third seal, I heard the third beast say, 'come and see.' And I beheld, and, lo, a black horse; and he that sat on him had a pair of balances in his hand. And I heard a voice in the midst of the four beasts say, A measure of wheat for a penny, and three measures of barley for a penny; and see thou hurt not the oil and the wine."—Rev. vi. 5, 6.

The next evangelist to whom I shall call your attention, is Mark. It is recorded in Mark xiii. 21: "And if any man shall say to you, lo, here is Christ; or, lo, he is there, believe him not." This quotation is part of a discourse of Christ to his disciples while seated upon the Mount of Olives, which refers to the destruction of Jerusalem, and includes ample directions to the disciples how to escape the severity of the calamities which was about to befall the Jewish nation. It is asserted that this passage is referred to, when the third seal is opened, and John heard the third beast say, "Come and see." For the word translated lo; as 'lo here;' lo there is the same word which is elsewhere translated see. And the phrase means see here, see there, and is equivalent to "come and see."

It is also asserted that the representation expressed by what John said he saw, is the same as the substance of the discourse of Christ to his disciples, which may be seen in the following manner: The black horse denotes famine, according to the usage of Scripture, as shown by Lam. v. 10: "Our skin was black like an oven, because of the terrible famine." The balances, or scales, in the hand of the rider on the black horse denotes the retribution which awaited the guilty victims, or the vengeance about to be inflicted upon the inhabitants of Jerusalem, for the rejection and crucifixion of our Savior. The scarcity of food and grain is indicated by the phrase "a measure of wheat for a penny, and three measures of barley for a penny." For the original word here translated measure denotes such a capacity as to contain the grain for the bread of one man one day; or, in modern military phraseology, one ration of wheat. For such a quantity to be sold for a denarius, the ancient Roman coin here translated penny, which was the wages of a man for a day, must denote great scarcity and high price. For, when a man can only earn in a day the bread required for himself for that day, it is evident he would have no surplus to buy food for a family, or to buy the other necessaries of life. And the starvation of all dependent on others for support, must be the natural consequence. And three measures of barley for a penny denotes that that grain was equally dear, considering the uses to which it was generally applied in ancient times, being appropriated to the sustenance of domestic animals; as wheat was to that of the human family. "And see thou hurt not the oil and the wine." In the parable of the ten virgins, the wise had oil in their vessels with their lamps. These evidently denote true Christians, as wine is used in the communion or Lord's supper, of which, those who properly partake, are true Christians.

The amount of the subject is this, that the destruction of Jerusalem was determined on, as a punishment to the disobedient Jews for their rejection and crucifixion of Christ; from which the Christians were to be exempt, as Christ had directed them that as a reward for their fidelity, and, also, that they might be instrumental in diffusing Christianity throughout the world. And the unbelieving Jews were to be deluded to their own destruction, by trusting in false Christs, who were expected to deliver them from the power of the Romans. But our Savior plainly foretold his disciples these events, and gave them such directions as enabled them personally to escape the calamities which befell their unbelieving countrymen. And this is the warning which is expressed by "lo, here is Christ; lo, he is there, believe them not." For, if they trusted in these false Christs, they would not obey the directions upon which their personal safety depended, and God would not interfere and furnish them other means to escape from the threatening calamity.

Although this discourse, on the Mount of Olives, was an explanation of a former one, predicting the destruction of the temple, it was, nevertheless, delivered at another time and place, and essentially distinct from it. For it was possible for the temple to be destroyed without the destruction of the city. And, also, for the latter to be mostly destroyed without the destruction of the former. They are two distinct things, inasmuch as each separately was a mystery or sealed subject to the Jews, and is, therefore, distinguished into two parts; namely, the destruction of the temple and its mode of worship, or the cessation of the Jewish religion as an object of divine appointment or favor, and the destruction of Jerusalem, under the most appalling scenes of bloodshed and famine.

Rev. vi. 7, 8: "And when he had opened the fourth seal, I heard the voice of the fourth beast say, 'come and see.' And I looked, and behold a pale horse: and his name that sat on him was death, and hell followed with him. And power was given unto them over the fourth part of the earth, to kill with sword, and with hunger, and with death, and with the beasts of the earth."

The next "come and see" that claims our attention, it seems, should be found in the book of Luke. Because I have quoted from John, Matthew, and Mark, and Luke, alone, remains. And I confess that I can not find any "come and see" in the book of Luke, corresponding with the representation set forth on the opening of the fourth seal. But I turn to the Acts of the Apostles, and find that it was written by an author, who had written another treatise of all that Jesus began to do and teach. And the Acts of the Apostles are generally attributed to Luke. And I find in Acts viii. 36, 37: "See, here is water; what doth hinder me to be baptized? And Philip said, if thou believest with all thine heart, thou mayest. And he answered and said, I believe that Jesus Christ is the Son of God." "See here" is a phrase equivalent to "come and see." And see, here is water, is connected with the confession that Jesus is the Christ. And when Peter made the same confession, Jesus told him that on this rock he would build his church. And it is a fact beyond the power of successful contradiction, that adherence to this confession was the cause of the death of Christ, and of all of his followers, who died as martyrs for his sake, as may be partly seen in Matt. xxvi. 63-66: "And the high priest answered and said unto him, I adjure thee by the living God, that thou tell us whether thou be the Christ the Son of God. Jesus saith unto him, Thou hast said: nevertheless, I say unto you, Hereafter shall ye see the Son of man sitting on the right hand of power, and coming in the clouds of heaven. Then the high priest rent his clothes, saying, He hath spoken blasphemy; what further need have we of witnesses? behold, now ye have heard his blasphemy. What think ye? They answered and said, He is guilty of death." Christ made this confession under oath before the Jewish high priest, and for it was judged guilty of blasphemy, and worthy of death. So, also, all of his disciples, who, by adhering to that confession, have sacrificed their lives, may be said to have perished by sword, and by hunger, and by the beasts of the earth.

The fourth seal opened reveals the fact which was before little understood, that God would permit the enemies of Christianity to show their hatred to it by their cruel persecutions of its early followers; and that he would make the malice of its enemies conducive to the spread of the gospel.

The opening of the fifth seal is not accompanied with references to passages in other parts of Scripture, but it shows that God's peculiar care was exercised toward those who had been martyred for the testimony which they held, although they had been cruelly treated by men in authority while on earth. That their persecution was not permitted from any want of love to their faithfulness, purity, and sincerity, but it was to test their fidelity, show the wonderful power of their faith, and perpetuate the purity of the church. That their reward was prepared and made sure unto them when their number should be completed.

Rev. vi. 12: "And I beheld when he had opened the sixth seal, and, lo, there was a great earthquake; and the sun became black as sackcloth of hair, and the moon became as blood." The word earthquake may, with equal propriety, be translated commotion. The elements of a physical revolution were organized which threatened the devastation and destruction of the established physical organization then existing. Clans and hoards of barbarians were organizing, gaining power, and making irruptions on civilized nations, threatening the devastation and destruction of the civilized governments, and the supplanting them by the hardships and privations of barbarian life

"And the sun became black as sackcloth of hair." This is interpreted as follows: The first equivalent for sun in the natural world is Christ the Sun of righteousness, who is so called spiritually or figuratively. Christ is called, in like manner, the "Word of God," and this last expression is susceptible of two interpretations, the latter of which signifies the Scriptures of truth, in which sense the connection requires it to be taken here. The Scriptures were, therefore, greatly depressed or overpowered by the disturbed state attending the barbarian invasion. For it was as sackcloth of hair, which denotes mourning; as sackcloth was used on such occasions. "And the moon became as blood," which is understood as follows: The moon denotes the ceremonial law of Moses—an institution inferior to the gospel. According as it it written: "The law was given by Moses, but grace and truth came by Jesus Christ. The law of Moses is compared with grace and truth, and is considered inferior to it. Grace and truth have been proved to be equal to the gospel, and

Christ and the gospel are used as equivalents, and Christ is the Sun of righteousness, therefore, the Sun of righteousness is compared with the law of Moses, and is acknowledged to be superior to it. And in the natural world, the light next inferior to the sun is the moon. Christ was the dispenser of the gospel as Moses was the law of Jewish ceremonies, and they stand in the same relation to each other as the sun does to the moon, which, therefore, denotes the ceremonial law of Moses, an institution enlightening mankind by its borrowed light. By becoming blood is to be understood the corruptive, dead state, to which it was reduced when superseded by the gospel.

Rev. vi. 13: "And the stars of heaven fell unto the earth, even as a fig-tree casteth her untimely figs, when she is shaken of a mighty wind."

The stars of heaven are the less lights of the firmament as the teachings of the apostles are inferior to that of Christ, the Sun of righteousness. They are also inferior to the law of Moses; inasmuch as they were not dignified with the rank of a separate institution of God, as was the Mosaic dispensation. These teachings were displaced or overwhelmed by the physical or natural commotion agitating the world; or, in other words, divinely appointed dispensations instituted by Moses. Christ and his apostles appeared to be overwhelmed by barbaric and Pagan idolatry.

Rev. vi. 14: "And the heaven departed as a scroll when it is rolled together; and every mountain and island were moved out of their places."

By the heaven departing as a scroll we are to understand that the events transpiring on the earth were apparently unfavorable to the reign of the Messiah or the gospel dispensation. That the kingdom of heaven or gospel dispensation retreated to the obscure places of earth. And as the mountains and islands are the prominent objects of earth and sea, so, also, the prominent objects in state and church were moved out of their accustomed abodes. For we have already shown that the word sea denotes the church, and what is earthly, if that is not which is not spiritual? Rev. vi. 15: "And the kings of the earth, and the great men, and the rich men, and the chief captains, and the mighty men, and every bond man, and every free man, hid themselves in the dens and in the rocks of the mountains."

All ranks and conditions of men were affected by this revolution, and greatly bewailed its dire calamities. They sought refuge from its severity in the huts and hovels of the barbarian; in the dens and caves of the earth— habitations more fit for the wild beasts of the wilderness, than for the abodes of civilized life. And, although inferior agencies were used to bring about those great changes in the affairs of men, yet the true cause was the wrath of the Lamb; or the retribution which awaited the persecutors of the Christian church.

Rev. viii. 1: "And when he had opened the seventh seal, there was silence in heaven about the space of half an hour."

The seventh seal differs from all the others in the number of the items of which it is composed, and the great length of time over which it extends. And it differs from the most of the others in being partly verified by a different witness. For the first five consist of only one item each. The first four are proved from the Scriptures, partly by means of the index "come and see." The fifth, sixth, and seventh are partly proved from the book of Providence, but they all agree in one particular, namely, in being illustrated by means of gospel equivalents, without which they are comparatively unintelligible. The seventh seal consists of seven distinct items, five of which are already past and finished. The sixth has been nearly completed, and the seventh item is yet to be developed in the future. Yet all these items can now be understood, although they are partly proved by different witnesses. For the Scriptures themselves are acknowledged to be sufficient testimony on any subject to which they relate. And the book of Providence or the history of the past transactions of men, when taken in connection with the testimony of inspiration is a reliable witness.

"There was silence in heaven about the space of half an hour." Between the administration of forbearance, and the retribution due to iniquity, a short pause took place, which is here indicated by the word silence. When Constantine, the Roman emperor, embraced Christianity, a day of temporal prosperity seemed about to dawn upon the church. We may suppose that great expectations were excited in the minds of all created holy intelligences, whether men or angels, to see the result of this change of the hostility of kings, heretofore manifested toward the church. A pause of suspense took place for a short duration, here designated by the term "silence for half an hour."

But the favor of kings was more detrimental to the church, than their most determined opposition. For the church persecuted was like gold tried in the fire. But the church protected by princes, became amalgamated with heathenish superstition. The world now became guilty of a two-fold sin against the church. It had been at first guilty of the most violent persecutions, and to this was added a more fearful consequence, namely, of corrupting the vital principles of truth and holiness. The silence mentioned in the text was the pause between the toleration of its enemies, who had inflicted terrible acts of injustice toward the church, and the retribution about to be inflicted upon the civilized world, in seven distinct particulars, and through many centuries of time.

The phrase "in heaven," in this place, is susceptible of two different interpretations. One is the church or gospel dispensation; as it is written, "For the kingdom of heaven is at hand." The other is the local habitation of the Deity, according as it is written, "Heaven is my throne." But in which ever sense it is here taken, it will not materially alter the meaning in this place, for in the former sense, the representation will have to be understood in the sense of announcement or prophecy. In the latter signification it will have to be understood of its design or determination. Prophecy or determination in the divine government are both equivalent to fulfillment or execution.

"And I saw the seven angels which stood before God." They are the same as the seven stars mentioned in Rev. i. 16, 20, wherein it is said the seven stars are the angels of the seven churches. The seven angels are the seven pastors of the churches of Asia. The word angel means messenger. God's messengers are most commonly disembodied spirits. But sometimes the sons of men are honored with the office of messenger; according as it is written, "For the priest's lips should keep knowledge, and they should seek the law at his mouth: for he is the messenger of the Lord of of hosts."—Mal. ii. 7. A pastor is the priest of the gospel dispensation, and a messenger is an angel. Things that are equal to the same are equal to each other. Therefore, the seven angels are the pastors of the seven churches of Asia.

"Which stood before God." The seven stars are represented to be held in Christ's right hand. He is represented as standing at the golden altar before the throne. And, moreover, Christ is represented in Rev. i. 13, as being in the midst of the seven golden candlesticks. And in verse twentieth, the seven candlesticks are declared to be the seven churches. A pastor's business and duties are with his flock or church. And if Christ was in the midst of the golden candlesticks, and his place was at the golden altar before the throne, and the seven stars were in his right hand, they, also, must be situated before the throne of God.

"And to them were given seven trumpets." The trumpet is an instrument of publication or proclamation; as is also a book. They are, therefore, equivalents. The seven trumpets are the seven copies of the book of Revelation, which John was commanded to write and send to the churches of Asia. According as it is written, "What thou seest write in a book and send unto the seven churches which are in Asia."—Rev. i. 11. They were to declare the contents of the book, like as if they proclaimed them with a trumpet. According as it is written in Isa. lviii. 1: "Cry aloud, spare not, lift up thy voice as a trumpet, and show my people their transgression, and the house of Jacob their sins."

Rev. viii. 3: "And another angel came and stood at the altar, having a golden censer; and there was given unto him much incense, that he should offer it with the prayers of all saints upon the golden altar which was before the throne." The golden censer, golden altar, and the incense with the prayers of all saints are the names of things and persons in both the Old and New Testaments. They, therefore, need not be solved by gospel equivalents.

CHAPTER V.

THE LAST SEVEN PLAGUES.

"AND I saw another sign in heaven, great and marvelous, seven angels having the seven last plagues; for in them is filled up the wrath of God."—Rev. xv. 1.

"And one of the four beasts gave unto the seven angels seven golden vials full of the wrath of God, who liveth forever and ever."—Rev. xv. 7.

"And I heard a great voice out of the temple saying to the seven angels, Go your ways, and pour out the vials of the wrath of God upon the earth."—Rev. xvi. 1.

The seven vials of God's wrath are said to be poured out upon the earth. It can be said that the word "earth" is not used strictly in the sense of the material earth in a philosophical sense. For the fourth vial was poured out upon the sun, which is no part of the earth, as one of the planets of the solar system. But the result of the outpouring of the fourth vial affected the inhabitants of the earth; for they were scorched with heat. It is plain that the word earth, in its first and general sense, is here used to designate the inhabitants of the earth, that is the earth which is the container is here used figuratively for its inhabitants; or, in other words, the fourth vial is said to be poured out upon the earth, when it is poured out upon the inhabitants. This figurative use of words is common to all mankind; as we say a man is wedded to his bottle—that is the liquor it contains; the stage dines here—that is the passengers.

THE LAST SEVEN PLAGUES.

God's final manifestations of displeasure toward the human race may be divided into seven different classes. The first one manifests that God vindicates the cause of the righteous by punishing in his own good time their oppressors. The second one makes it evident that spiritual advantages, if neglected and perverted, shall be taken from their possessors, and given to others who will make better use of those privileges. The third makes it evident, that if they pervert the ordinances of God's worship, that he permits them to know, by bitter experience, that they will receive less advantages from false systems of theology than from true ones. The fourth one shows that if they practice evil, while acknowledging the authority of the Word of God, they must pervert its interpretation to justify their conduct. The fifth shows that God often makes use of perverted beings to punish others of like character. The sixth shows that God has great care over the free investigation of the Scriptures, and will not always permit them to be bound, but will cut off from the living those that circumscribe its free investigation. The seventh shows that God will eventually bring into contempt and derision all kinds of false philosophy which comes in contact with his word.

The first of the last seven plagues was national in its character, warlike in its nature, and deteriorating in its results. It was the martial triumph of barbarism over civilization. In this respect it differed from some of the triumphs of preceding ages, which had resulted in planting a more intelligent and scientific civilization on the minds of a ruder, more indolent and barbarous one, as the erection of the Grecian empire was the triumph of superior skill and energy over indolence and luxury. For the Greeks excelled the Persians in general intelligence and enterprise, as well as military science and energy of character. The Roman empire, also, was founded by military skill, as well as by a superiority of valor and hardihood. But the overthrow of this empire was the triumph of a rude valor over a refined indolence. For the Romans, in the decline of their empire, retained refinements of scientific skill without their original hardihood of character. These attainments proved inadequate to the desperate valor of the barbarians. The result of the seven barbarian invasions was the downfall of the Roman empire, and formed a new epoch in the history of nations. In an earthly point of view, this is viewed as a calamity, and this result is by the writer considered as the first of the last seven plagues. It was an act of retribution dispensed upon a guilty, idolatrous nation, which had shamefully persecuted the servants of the Most High, who now had in his providence commenced a series of chastisements to teach rebellious men moderation and equity, and to do his saints no harm.

Is it not plainly perceptible that the refinements of luxury chiefly tend to bodily ease and comfort? For, who would willingly relinquish the advantages of a commodious and comfortable dwelling for the rude hut of the barbarian or savage? Would not the lodge of the Indian, made of poles and covered with skins or bark, admitting wind and rain, and only partially emitting smoke from a hole in the roof, be considered more desirable than the splendid mansion with all its implements of art and luxury? Would the mahogany sofa and downy bed be willingly substituted for the ground and puncheon floor, covered with leaves or skins of wild animals, for a couch by day or a bed by night? Would the precarious fare of the hunter or fisherman be willingly exchanged for the luxurious repast of modern cookery? If there is plainly a difference in these modes of life, the advantages belong to a state of civilization and refinement. If God in his providence should cause the overthrow of this civilization, he might justly be said to pour out his wrath upon the bodily ease and comfort of men. And, accordingly, the first vial was said to be poured out upon the earth, or the bodies of men, when the wars which it predicted resulted most disastrously to the ease and comfort of the individuals who suffered its calamity.

The sixteenth chapter of the book of Revelation contains an account of the outpouring of the seven vials of God's wrath. It is recorded in Rev. xvi. 1, 2: "And I heard a great voice out of the temple saying to the seven angels, Go your ways, and pour out the vials of the wrath of God upon the earth. And the first went, and poured out his vial upon the earth; and there fell a noisome and grievous sore upon the men which had the mark of the beast, and upon them which worshiped his image."

The science of scriptural algebra, like algebra itself, is applied to the investigation of things unknown. The proper use of gospel equivalents consists in simply substituting, in some instances, equivalent gospel expressions for one another. For example in the pouring out of the vials recorded in Rev. xvi., I merely substitute some equivalent for the object upon which it was poured, taking all other parts of the description in their most obvious and acknowledged meanings. The first angel poured out his vial upon the earth. The word earth is not to be taken in its inanimate form, but to be substituted for the bodies of men. As it is written, "dust thou art," and as it is said in the burial service, "earth to earth, and dust to dust." The theory is, that God was about to execute signal vengeance upon the civilized world for their persecution of the church. And so he had prepared the northern barbarians to overthrow the Roman empire, and obliterate civilization with its genial physical developments. For who will deny that civilization is more conducive to bodily ease and comfort than a state of barbarism? So, then, the first vial was poured out upon the earth, or the bodies of men, when the Roman empire was displaced by northern barbarism.

Nor is it a valid objection to this theory because it is recorded in the second verse of the same chapter, that "there fell a noisome and grievous sore upon the men which had the mark of the beast, and upon them which worshiped his image." Admitting that the characters described as having the marks of the beast, and as being worshipers of his image, were not in existence when the Roman empire was destroyed, the results of the first vial poured out did not terminate with the first objects of God's displeasure. For the substitution of barbarism for civilization was not only detrimental to the bodily ease and enjoyment of its first victims, but was also detrimental to Christian light and knowledge, and was attended with mental degradation, ignorance, superstition, and many other concomitant evils. And the adherents of the apostate church, in after ages, also felt the evils attendant on an obliterated civilization. Their calamity was not of the same kind as that of the first objects of God's displeasure, but was, nevertheless, the natural consequence of the manifestation of that displeasure.

Rev. xvi. 3: "And the second angel poured out his vial upon the sea; and it became as the blood of a dead man: and every living soul died in the sea."

Although the effect of the second vial poured out was partly produced by the pouring out of the first; yet God had not relinquished his providential care of his intelligent creatures. He did not, in this instance, permit its direful effects to fall upon the innocent. For he doth nothing without a cause. According as it is written in Prov. xxvi. 2: "The curse causeless shall not come."

In the solution of the book of Revelation by the system I have adopted, the object upon which the second vial was poured out is not so plainly obvious as are the objects upon which the other vials are poured, but the connection with the other vials and concurrent circumstances conspire to prove it to be the professing church of Christ, which had apostatized from the true faith. It may not be considered a violation of sound interpretation to consider the phrase translated many waters, in the first verse of chapter seventeen, equivalent to the word sea in this. For the phrase might, with propriety, be translated "much water," which is the natural equivalent for the sea. If this should be admitted to be so, we have given us, by divine inspiration, the interpretation of many waters to be peoples, and multitudes, and nations, and tongues of which the visible church, whether of Christ or antichrist, was composed. For the church is composed of individual members of different nations and languages. Nor are the points of resemblance few or unimportant. The sea, like the church, receives the refuse and impurities of earth, and purifies them. They both have received constant accessions in all ages of the world, and from all parts of the earth, and yet there is room in each. The sea is salt, and true Christians are the salt of the earth. The church is composed of the human family, and the sound of men, in the busy haunts of life, resembles the sound of many waters. The sea possesses the elements of self-preservation, as does also the church. So, then, it is maintained that the sea, the object upon which the second vial was poured out, was the nominal church of Christ.

Now, the history of events in question is, that the barbarians overthrew the civilization of the world, and the nominal church of Christ became corrupted by receiving into it unworthy members, who did not partake of, appreciate, or understand the purity of its design or origin.

Rev. xvi. 4: "And the third angel poured out his vial upon the rivers and fountains of waters; and they became blood."

The third vial was poured out upon the rivers and fountains of waters. By rivers and fountains of waters we are to understand something like ordinances of religion, or principles of Christianity. According as it is written: "And he showed me a pure river of water of life, clear as crystal, proceeding out of the throne of God and the Lamb."—Rev. xxii. 1. "And let him that is athirst come. And whosoever will, let him take the water of life freely."—Rev. xxii. 17. By blood is to be understood pollution. According as it is written in Ezek. xvi. 6: "And when I passed by thee, and saw thee polluted in thine own blood." The ordinances of Christianity, like the apostle himself, are a savor of life unto life, or death unto death. According to the declaration of the apostle as found recorded in Cor. ii. 15, 16: "For we are unto God a sweet savor of Christ, in them that are saved, and in them that perish. To the one we are the savor of death unto death, and to the other the savor of life unto life." So, then, when the apostate church polluted the ordinances of Christianity, they became an abomination in the sight of God, and became the instruments of condemnation, instead of the means of grace And the third vial of God's wrath may be said to be poured out upon them when they had totally lost their life-giving efficacy.

Rev. xvi. 8: "And the fourth angel poured out his vial upon the sun; and power was given unto him to scorch men with fire."

And the fourth vial was poured out upon the sun. By the word sun is to be understood the Scriptures of truth, which are shown to be the equivalents in the following manner: Christ is generally acknowledged to be the Sun of righteousness. He is also called the Word of God, according as it is written in Rev. xix. 13: " And he was clothed with a vesture dipped in blood: and his name is called the Word of God." But the phrase "Word of God" denotes, also, the Scriptures of truth. Does any one maintain that we have no authority for the substitution of the word Scriptures for the word Christ as the signification of the phrase Word of God. For the benefit of such, I will prove that this virtually corresponds with the usage of the Scriptures. For the word Christ is, by the usage of the Scriptures, considered equivalent to the word gospel, which latter word I will prove by the peculiarities of scriptural algebra equivalent to the entire "Word of God;" although, in so doing, I shall be compelled to explain some principles of scriptural algebra not otherwise necessary to the elucidation of the subject. To preach Christ is to preach the gospel, and the latter is the most essential part of the Scriptures, and can not be fully illustrated and established without the writings of all other parts of the Old and New Testaments. The gospel is like the vital parts of the human or any other animal body, which being destroyed the animal life is destroyed with them. So, also, it is written the Scriptures can not be broken. Nor was Christ's bones broken on the cross. For it is written in Heb. iv. 12: "The Word of God is quick, powerful, and sharper than any two-edged sword, piercing even to the dividing asunder of soul and spirit, and of the joints and marrow."

The soul is the life and the spirit is the intention. The Scriptures make a distinction between the gospel, which is the life of the Scriptures and the spirit or intention of other parts, some of which were written for different purposes. And a distinction should also be observed between the joint and marrow. For as it is possible to enter into life halt or maimed, rather than having two hands or two feet to be cast into hell fire. So, also, in the living body, a man may have his hand or foot severed from the body without the destruction of his life. But the destruction of the spinal marrow would cause death. The word quick means living, and the Scriptures observe the laws of animate nature. In inanimate nature, to which the principles of common algebra are adapted, the whole is equal to all the parts, and all the parts are equal to the whole. But in animate nature, to which the principles of scriptural algebra are adapted, the chief part is equal to the whole, and the whole is equal to the chief part. For, destroy the head, heart or spinal marrow in the human body, and the life of the body becomes extinct. So, also, the gospel bears the same relation to the rest of the Scriptures as the seat of life does in animate nature, that is take it away and life becomes extinct. I have proved or have it granted that the word Christ is equivalent to the Sun of righteousness, or the sun itself, the phrase Word of God and the gospel. Therefore, they are severally equivalent to each other; according to the mathematical axiom, things which are equal to the same are equal to each other. And I have also shown that the gospel is equivalent to all the Scriptures, because all parts of the sacred writings are necessary to its development. Nor is the sun an unsuitable representative of the Scriptures of truth. For as the sun in the natural world is the source of light, heat, and vitality, so, also, the Scriptures or the gospel in the spiritual world is the source of light, life and the fervor of devotion. The fourth vial was, therefore, poured out upon the Scriptures. That is, their true interpretation became corrupted; for how could a degenerate church receive unworthy members, and corrupt the ordinances of Christianity, and give their true interpretation in condemnation of their conduct. They must, therefore, invent false interpretations to justify themselves. According as it is written: "And even as they did not like to retain God in their knowledge, God gave them over to a reprobate mind, to do those things which are not convenient."—Rom. i. 28. They must, therefore, invent false interpretations to justify themselves. And from these false interpretations sprang the inquisition which persecuted with the sword and fagot, tortured them in dungeons, and burnt them at the stake. So, then, was the prophecy fulfilled that power was given unto the sun to scorch men with fire.

Rev. xvi. 10, 11: " And the fifth angel poured out his vial upon the seat of the beast; and his kingdom was full of darkness; and they gnawed their tongues for pain. And blasphemed the God of heaven, because of their pains and their sores, and repented not of their deeds."

The Mahometan power was raised up as a scourge of the kingdoms occupying the territory which formerly belonged to the Roman empire in its brightest days of earthly glory. The conquests of the Saracens were limited on the west at the Pyrenees mountains by the successful valor of Charles Martel, a Christian warrior of distinction and renown. And their repeated attacks on Constantinople, on the east, were equally unsuccessful. This city was the capital of the eastern empire, which was under the jurisdiction of the Greek church. The northern part of Africa and the European dominions of Rome, the seven-hilled city, were the scenes of their devastations, pillage, and slaughter. They were, therefore, emphatically a scourge of those inhabiting the seat of the beast—the great red dragon, having seven heads and ten horns. But this providential chastisement of the Almighty failed to accomplish its intended beneficial results. They did not renounce their cherished corruptions, and return to the true worship of God.

Rev. xvi. 12, 13, 16: "And the sixth angel

poured out his vial upon the great river Euphrates; and the water thereof was dried up, that the way of the kings of the east might be prepared. And I saw three unclean spirits like frogs come out of the mouth of the dragon, and out of the mouth of the beast, and out of the mouth of the false prophet. And he gathered them together into a place called in the Hebrew tongue Armageddon."

The river Euphrates was the cause of the greatness of Imperial Babylon, because rivers have always been selected as eligible places near which to build large cities, and as Babylon represents the apostate church, as New Jerusalem does also the church of Christ, the sixth vial was, therefore, poured out upon that which constituted the greatness of the Apostate church. And what else constituted its greatness but the assumptions of divine authority? Its false pretentions and assumptions were the object of God's displeasure and vengeance. And in disturbing the blasphemous pretensions of this church, the way was prepared for the true interpretation of the Scriptures, and the reception of the true Messiah, whose original advent upon the earth was welcomed by the wise men of the east, who adored him, and presented him with kingly gifts, gold, frankincense, and myrrh. But this introduction of a better era was not effected without violent opposition. The unreasonable sources of wrath were opposed against this reformation.

That the way has been prepared by the pouring out of the sixth vial for the extension of the knowledge of the Scriptures among mankind may be seen from the following views of the interposition of Divine Providence among the nations of the earth. The war in China, in 1848, between the British and the Chinese governments, resulted favorably to the English, although the object of the Chinese, which was to suppress the ruinous sale and smuggling of opium, was justifiable. It may be that, in desiring to accomplish that object, they deviated from moderation and equity, yet their design was commendable. For it was exceedingly expensive as well as injurious to the health of the inhabitants. The result of this war was to continue the sale of opium as well as other commodities, and to open the ports of several cities to the commerce of Great Britain. The effect of this new settlement of the difficulties was to prepare the way for the greater diffusion of knowledge, and of the Christian religion into that extensive empire, which is supposed to contain about one-third of the population of the world.

The late great rebellion in China, which had for its object the expulsion of the Tartar dynasty and the restoration of the native Chinese to power, had a tendency to open still wider the gates of the Celestial empire, as it is called, to the diffusion of knowledge, the extension of arts and commerce, and the spread of the gospel. So that such signal defeats and revolutions in the most populous empire in the world seem to be the work of God in preparing the way for the spread of the gospel. So that good and wise men have not hesitated to attribute it to his beneficial work.

A spiritual conflict is progressing on the

earth for the extension of Christian knowledge and the means of grace among the inhabitants of the earth. And to make the termination of this conflict favorable to the reign of the Redeemer's kingdom, God has overruled, and still continues to overrule, the evil passions of men to accomplish his benevolent purposes among men. As another instance of the interposition of Divine Providence in the affairs of men, and of his using their military preparations to accomplish his own purposes, I might refer you to the present result and future prospects gained by the suppression of the late rebellion in our own country. The slaveholder's rebellion in the United States has had a tendency to elevate the African race in this country. It has abolished those local restrictions in the slave states against the education of the negroes. And, although of itself, it has not created schools nor supported teachers; yet it has prepared the way for all who are favorably disposed to extend in that direction the sphere of their usefulness. But the influence of the late civil war in America was not confined to the United States or even Europe; for this war affected the commerce and industry of the world. The great demand for raw cotton stimulated the production of that commodity in the distant provinces of the British in India. And the tendency of a greater social intercourse of the British with their Asiatic provinces, has been to elevate the moral and intellectual condition of the natives of that country. And the past and the present condition of Mexico has a tendency to encourage Protestant emigration from the United States into Catholic Mexico. Many of these emigrants carry with them the leaven of Protestantism, which may eventually leaven the whole lump of the Mexican nation.

Rev. xvi. 17: "And the seventh angel poured out his vial into the air; and there came a great voice out of the temple of heaven, from the throne, saying, it is done."

Rev. xvi. 18: "And there were voices, and thunders, and lightnings; and there was a great earthquake, such as was not since men were upon the earth, so mighty an earthquake, and so great."

The sixth vial portrayed national calamities, in which individuals suffered but only as component parts of the nations. The seventh vial portrays individual calamities directly of a moral and intellectual kind, and indirectly attended with the loss of pecuniary honors and emoluments. The seventh vial may be said figuratively to create an overseer over all the channels of the communication of ideas. Whatever is in accordance with the Word of God will become honorable and approved. And whatever shall not be in accordance therewith shall be held in contempt and derision. And then will be speedily carried out the declaration: "He that honoreth me will I honor, and he that despiseth me shall be lightly esteemed." And this supervision shall extend to all the intellectual labors of the human race without regard to the intentions of individuals, and be directed by the infallible decisions of the divine mind. The interpretation of the Scriptures will be reduced to a mathematical certainty. Intellectual giants will appear and carry the banner of inspiration from one victory to another, until every thing in science and philosophy incompatible with the Word of God will be routed and scouted from respectable society.

"And the seventh angel poured out his vial into the air." Wind in the natural world is air put in motion. Wind or air puffeth up; as we can fill bladders with wind or air. It is also recorded in 1 Cor. viii. 1: "Knowledge puffeth up," which, of course, must be understood to refer to false knowledge, or as it is otherwise described by the apostle Paul as philosophy falsely so called: "Beware lest any man spoil you through philosophy and vain deceit."—Col. ii. 8. The conclusion of the matter is this, that air in the natural world is the gospel equivalent for false philosophy in the moral and intellectual world. And the seventh vial of God's wrath is poured out into the air when it is poured out upon false philosophy. But it may be said, how can that be a plague which must inevitably be a general blessing to the church and the world. To this it is replied that a partial evil may be a general good. So, also, it is written in 1 Cor. iii. 12, 15: "Now if any man build upon this foundation gold, silver, precious stones, wood, hay, stubble. If any man's work shall be burned, he shall suffer loss." The interpretation of the prophecy relating to the outpouring of the seventh vial makes that event almost entirely, yet in the future. And consequently it can be proved only by the tesmony of one witness, namely, the book of inspiration. I shall not, therefore, pretend that this vial can now be fully explained in all its minute details. This I have not even attempted to do in interpreting the six which are already or almost entirely past. For this simple reason, that the time allotted to one individual, burdened with domestic cares, and deprived of many facilities of investigation are too brief for so stupendous a task. I have, therefore, come to a conclusion of the subject, and submit the matter for the candid consideration of the religious world.

CONCLUSION.

I HAVE completed the present writing on the last seven plagues. The subject is not exhausted, nor are all the difficulties overcome. For it is written in Rev. xv. 8: "And the temple was filled with smoke from the glory of God, and from his power; and no man was able to enter into the temple, till the seven plagues of the seven angels were fulfilled." It should be noticed that the text does not say no man was able to see into the temple, but that no man was able to enter there. But it may not be amiss to inquire what is meant by the word temple. The Jewish temple was the local habitation of the Deity. Christ compared his body to the Jewish temple, when he said, "Destroy this temple, and in three days I will rear it again." It is, therefore, a gospel equivalent by comparison. But Christ is called the Word of God, which also means the Scriptures of truth. As the temple is the equivalent for Christ, which is also the equivalent for the Word of God, temple and Word of God must be equivalent. For things that are equal to the same are equal to each other.

Although it is not possible now to enter the temple of truth or fully understand all the prophecies of Scripture, because the seventh vial is not fully poured out, yet, at the commencement of the outpouring of that vial, the smoke begins to disappear from the temple, and we are able to see into it. As Moses, the servant of God, could see the promised land of Canaan, although he was not permitted to enter therein. Especially is this the case in this instance, because it is also written in Rev. x. 7: "But in the days of the days of the voice of the seventh angel, when he shall begin to sound, the mystery of God should be finished as he has declared to his servants the prophets." By this last prophecy, I understand that all obstacles heretofore placed in the way of a proper understanding or elucidation of the subject will be removed by the interposition of Divine Providence. And the subject thereafter will yield to human investigation and persevering study. I do not expect, under the most favorable circumstances, to be able to fathom all the mysteries of the Apocalypse. In his own suitable time, the Lord will raise up the proper men to accomplish that work. But what I do expect to accomplish is to show to the world that it is possible to explain that book in a consistent, intelligible, and reliable manner, to the understandings of all men, whether learned or unlearned.

Nor do I expect to accomplish this without divine assistance. For God has reserved the honor of that discovery to himself. The battle is not to the strong, nor the revelation to the most profound in biblical attainments. According as it is written in Matt. xi. 25, 26: "I thank thee, O Father, Lord of heaven and earth, because thou hast hid these things from the wise and prudent, and hast revealed them unto babes. Even so, Father; for so it seemed good in thy sight." Accordingly, the primary cause of all my efforts in studying, speaking, and writing on the book of Revelation was the following dream. I dreamed that I was in the New Jerusalem. That I was disappointed in finding it an earthly city instead of a heavenly one. That I was in a room of a house of an ordinary appearance in which I saw men and women dressed differently. That I noticed one woman in particular who was dressed in a common calico dress, having a pale countenance. That I asked why she looked so pale, and was informed the reason was that she might be known. And that I saw in the room a barrel resembling a flour barrel about half full of fruit, about the size of a large peach or a small apple as bright as gold. Then I awoke and found it was a dream. The subject, I doubt not, will meet the scrutiny of the learned and unlearned. For God's mysterious providence hovers over my path, making me willing, in the day of his power, to risk the necessary pecuniary means, and to forego the ease and comforts of home, in order to spread a knowledge of my investigations among the hovels of the poor, and the mansions of the wise and great. The sympathy of mankind will be excited in my behalf, and cause them to buy the book from motives of humanity as well as from a sense of religious duty. And when the end designed is accomplished, I trust the affliction will be removed, and we will all rejoice in the mercy as we now grieve under the power of God.

Some may scoff at the idea of the interposition of Divine Providence in this age of the world, and suppose that such interpositions were confined to the Jews, the chosen people of God in the Old Testament dispensation, and to the apostles and evangelists of the New. They may obliterate from their own memories, but they can not blot out from the pages of history the record of such interpositions. The history of Cyrus the Great is recorded by Heroditus and Justin, as well as by the words of inspiration. The dream of his grandfather Astyages, its interpretation by the wise men of that time, and the means used to defeat it, are all a matter of history. The dream, according to the interpretation of the wise men, predicted the birth of a grandson, who would dethrone his grandfather, and conquer all Asia. Astyages took measures to defeat this catastrophy, by even plotting the exposure of the child to a cruel death. But the devices of men proved unavailing, and, in the hands of God, the means of its fulfillment. So, also, Alexander the Great was inspired with his extraordinary courage, perseverance, and unbounded ambition, by a dream inviting him to come over and conquer Asia. And when the Jewish high priest met him with a supplicating train beseeching his clemency and forbearance, the great conqueror acknowledged the fulfillment of the dream, and conferred upon the suppliants the blessings they sought. Need I add that Julius Cæsar and Bonaparte also believed in a Divine Providence, or predetermined destiny. If such men as these were raised up to accomplish some purposes predicted in the divine record, is it absurd to sup-

CONCLUSION. 117

pose that the prophecies relating to the Millennium will not be fulfilled by the interposition of Divine Providence in the affairs of men. I trust there will be few intelligent Christians willing to controvert this position.

And the question only remains whether the means proposed are adequate to so stupendous a task as the unfolding the mysteries of the Apocalypse, or ushering in the light which shall illuminate the world in the Millennial day.

The author of this book contends that the science of scriptural algebra, when fully and universally understood, is competent to the task. He has given practical examples of the solution of some problems by means of this science, without explaining those principles in a formal manner. Necessity required this method in order to be understood.

The principle of the substitution of equivalents is so obvious that many suppose they have always practiced it. Perhaps such persons do not know the trials and experiments which the author has used to come at these conclusions. The principles of a science are often learned as well by trying examples in which the solution is not solved, as in those which are. It is reserved for another occasion, and the publication of another book, to treat the subject in a more formal and scientific manner. Perhaps, on the examination of some of the curious results of this science, some people might be better prepared to judge whether they have always practiced these principles in exactly the same manner.

But I will bring my book to a close by answering one objection, which, I suppose, will be asked. If the principle of the substitution of equivalents is so obvious as to appear almost inherent in the human mind, how has it happened that the extension and scientific arrangement of this principle should have been overlooked. It can only be accounted for on the supposition that God ordained it so to be. According to the declaration of inspiration recorded in Rev. x. 1: "And I saw another mighty angel come down from heaven, clothed with a cloud." And this prophecy of the vision of John was fulfilled by those changes and obliterations of the learning of antiquity when those libraries, which contained the scientific attainments of the ancient nations of the world, were destroyed by fire, during the wars of the barbarians and Saracens with the civilized world. Thus verifying the declaration, he doeth his will among the armies of heaven, and among the inhabitants of the earth.

www.ingramcontent.com/pod-product-compliance
Lightning Source LLC
Chambersburg PA
CBHW020130170426
43199CB00010B/712